To my dear and wonderful Dad —
thanks for blessing me with an appreciation
for family! Hope you enjoy reading
about other fathers and their children -- and
know that you are the best Dad for me."

Love,
Shell

Also by **Bill Hanson**:

father&son: The Bond

A Shoulder to Lean On

Photography by

Bill Hanson
Author of **father&son**

Photographs and essays
celebrating fathers with their children.

Library of Congress Catalog Number: 97-94235

ISBN 1-880092-42-5

Edited by Peggy Fikac

Designed by Lynne Henderlong-Rhea

Digital imaging and scanning by CMYK Pre-Press
Printed in Canada

First Edition

12 11 10 9 8 7 6 5 4 3 2 1

Bright Books

P.O. Box 50335

Austin, Texas 78763-0335

512-499-4164

Fax 512-477-9975

To those who joyfully and unselfishly give of themselves,

lending an ear, serving as a rock—always a shoulder to lean on.

CONTENTS

CONTENTS *Continued*

ACKNOWLEDGMENTS

- First and foremost. I would like to thank all the fathers and children for your enthusiasm. time. and willingness to be in the book: I'm honored to know you and in return honor you with this tribute. Thanks for opening your hearts. and may the world be touched by your words.
- Peggy Fikac for working on deadline and your oneness with the written word.
- Lynne Henderlong-Rhea. for being so devoted to the integrity of the book's design.
- Evan and Julia Smith. for your wonderful bedside manner as word docs.
- Jan Pearce. Director of Travel. "I must have exit row for legroom."
- Beth Borgman. the tenacious one—thanks for your unwavering energy.
- To all the people who helped me with the shoots and the production of the book. and friends and family who believed in my message and encouraged and supported me when I lost my objectivity: Alfred McEwen. Anya Hanson. Arielle Ford. Austin Prints for Publication. Betts Skye. Chaz Corzine. CJ Douglas. Colom and Gina Keating—Bite Me!. Darryl Wimberley. Dean Johnson. Gary Duncan. Joe Lupariello. Jon and Kathleen Hanson. Kent Waldrep. Kitty Thomas. Layton Blalock. Marilyn Christian. Marty Kazen—for your support and enduring my myopic vision. Melissa Schenker. Mitch Stoller. Mom and Stan. Nancy Hamilton Bowman. Nicole Dunigan. Rich Thurber. Terrie Miller. Trevor "Sulpulveda" Romain. Virgil Robbins. the crew at CMYK—"Pixelate."

My deepest appreciation and gratitude to Christopher Reeve and his family for their time and participation in this book. I'm inspired by your strength and internal fortitude to pursue your dreams through such adversity.

A Shoulder to Lean On is a message of the power of love. hope. and family. It will benefit the nonprofit organization. the National Paralysis Foundation. to provide major media exposure and to raise awareness of the many needs of people afflicted with paralysis. The goal is to find a cure. once and for all. Researchers are intensely studying the mechanisms by which the brain and spinal cord recover from injury. These studies have shown that the brain and spinal cord possess a remarkable capacity to recover from severe injury. As Christopher Reeve says. "Now we stand on the threshold of full recovery. It can happen. The scientists are ready. willing. and able. With support. they will do it."

One dollar from each book sold will be donated to the National Paralysis Foundation to help make the dream of walking come true.

"**D**addy," my five-year-old son, Miles, tells me, "I have a secret to tell you." I lean down to give him my ear and my full attention. "You are my best friend," he says.

A little piece of me melts as the words leave his mouth. "That's right," I reply. "And you are my best friend too, buddy." I get a big bear hug and a wide jack-o'-lantern smile. My heart fills up. Miles may not be old enough to understand it, but I'm proud and honored to be his father and friend. He wants me to be his hero too, and I'm up to that challenge. *He* is *my* hero.

From the moment your child takes his first fitful breath, your life ceases to be about *you*. Your life is given over in that moment to prepare an infant boy or girl for a future that will always remain, except in the broadest outlines, unknowable. No job demands more of us than this preparation for uncertainty. And the labor never ends.

Parenting is a non-stop enterprise. We parents have a constant responsibility for the well-being and happiness of our children—every minute, every hour, every day, every week, every year. At the minimum we enter a covenant, even at conception, that obligates us to give our children the tools they need to survive.

As parents, we have seen sickness and uncertainty and failure and know they can't be avoided. So we guide our children past every thorn, tear, and cavity, every Little League strikeout or piano recital with the constant refrain: Don't worry. Hang in there. It'll work out.

It doesn't always work out, of course. And that is the parent's agony, to give hope and consolation knowing that our children will have setbacks. There is no life without some tragedy. But with a parent's calm compass a child can endure an incredible array of experience. Fathers, especially, are uniquely charged to combine challenge and discipline with empathy and compassion. You can hit that ball if you work hard enough. You can master that concerto, hit that serve, swim that lake. You can, you can, you can, a father tells his child. And then he says, after success or through failure, "It's all right. I love you. I won't go away. No matter what."

We've always recognized the mother's place in parenting, and we always should. As I say in my first book, *Father & Son: The Bond*, I consider the relationship between mother and child equally significant. But we know now that fathers have an irreplaceable role to play in the lives of their children. A father's shoulders are built to be firmly leaned on.

Being a father is the hardest job you'll ever have, but it's also the best. By spending time with my son, I am creating a shared language of trust, respect, empathy, and instruction, helping Miles to know who he is and fostering a relationship that will nourish us both for all the days of our never-separate lives.

A Shoulder to Lean On is a celebration of this relationship between father and child, child and father. It is a heartfelt tribute in words and pictures to the bonds we forge, the respect we share, and a love that never dies. Each father-and-child team in this book has found a common denominator in their relationship. On the following pages you will journey through the awesome, yet insightful, shifting sands of parenthood.

Society is never going to raise a better class of men without raising a better class of fathers. We pay too high a cost for fathers who run out on the job. A child may know the reason why his father isn't around, but he'll never understand it. What he will do too often is to mimic the pattern of parenting that he sees, fueling a cycle of fatherlessness that is bad for families and bad for society.

That cycle stops when men take fathering seriously. By playing a vital role in the life of their children, fathers become better citizens and much better men. As a single father I take special pride in the amount of time I spend with my son. Fathers, on average, do not take nearly enough time to be with their children.

Many men would love to play a more active role in their children's lives, but the workplace's cards are stacked against it. All across the country, men are not seriously being encouraged to focus less on work and more on their families. Society tends to look skeptically at men who want to take paternity leave or time off for anything else that is not career oriented. I see that there is a change in the expectations we place on these issues concerning parenting and lifestyles in general. What will the changes bring?

I have made a decision to forgo some business opportunities so that my son can be my highest priority. It takes quite a bit of reorganizing on a daily basis to keep that priority, but I'm committed to Miles first, then to my work. I don't judge myself by the title I hold or the salary I earn, by the house I own or the car I drive. My self-esteem, my sense of manhood, in fact, is based on how well I perform as a father. Happiness for me is derived from the happiness of my son. After all, what else really matters?

When you *do* want to be there and when you make time to be there, marvelous things can happen. My dad had to make trips when I was little. He took me along. I'll never forget those times, driving down the open highway, sitting on his lap. I'd pretend to drive. He'd pretend to let me. I was so happy being with my dad. Staying with him in the motels near the highways. Listening to the *whoooooosh* of eighteen-wheelers framed by those amber lights, heading for a destination shrouded in mystery.

Of course, children do things you don't expect. One night I got up from my motel bed and sleepwalked out of our room. By the time I realized I was outside, I was disoriented. I had no idea where my room was. I was afraid to start knocking on doors that all looked alike. I stumbled on our car, finally, and knelt by the tire hoping Dad would wake and save me from whatever terrible things lurked in that dark and scary parking lot.

Dad did find me. He must have been terrified, waking to find me gone. But he didn't convey any of that fear to me. Nor anger, either. "What about it, little buddy?" I looked up from the smell of asphalt and rubber to see a familiar silhouette bent over the frame of our car. "Daddy!" I cried. He scooped me up and cradled my head against his shoulder.

"I'm sorry, Daddy!"

"It's awright, Billy," he squeezed me tight. "Everybody takes a little walk now and then."

Memories like these are all I have of my father now. Dad died suddenly in 1980. I'll never forget that phone call, "Bill, we've lost your dad." At first I didn't understand.

"I haven't seen him around here," I replied to the caller. After all, everybody takes a little walk now and then.

Fortunately, my father made sure he made many memories for me to keep. When the funeral came, I decided not to look at his body. I wanted to keep his face alive in the memory that survived. I wanted to have in my heart the presence of a close and loving and never-dying relationship. My brother, in contrast, was younger and had not spent as much time with Dad. When he came to me after viewing our father, he collapsed in my arms, heartbroken.

On those wonderful open-highway drives my dad used to say, "Don't look into the sun, Bill." I have a son of my own now; I don't need to look anywhere else. He warms my heart, and in his eyes I am overwhelmed by a bright and abiding love—just as every father should be.

"Holding On — Letting Go..."

December 22, 1980

It's a girl...gorgeous...red hair. She's bright, funny.

I'm playing Oklahoma honky-tonks, living on pipe dreams.

I hold her all the time.

January 22, 1997

43 years old.

I'm fighting to keep my baby girl.

She's fighting to be a woman.

She wants to drive, date BOYS!

I'm gone 100 days a year. I'm too controlling. It's so hard to let go! I need more time.

Don't leave, slow down.

HEY! I love you. I'm trying...WAIT!

July 12, 1983

It's a boy...complications with labor leave fluid in his lungs. I'm caught up in portraying the strong man and fight back the emotion that almost chokes me.

I worry about both mother and son. I break down alone at home, nobody knows. It's what I learned from my dad, "a man's man," and he learned it from his dad.

January 22, 1997

It's okay to cry...show pain...emotion...to touch, hug. Tell him that I love him. He'll be strong. He's kind, gentle, patient, a good teacher. He'll be a good man.

October 28, 1994

A miracle...Janine's not supposed to have children. After six years of marriage, lightning strikes. It's girl! Again, gorgeous...redhead. A mile a minute, angel of joy. Always laughing loud, completely uninhibited, just like her mother. I cry, I laugh. I try to be less controlling, more patient.

It's slow, tedious, and sometimes frightening, but I guess it is for all kids raising a dad!

CECE WINANS *Daughter /* | **DAVID WINANS** *Father*

Singer / Songwriter

A father is a daughter's first impression of a man. This relationship often determines her relationships with men throughout her life—her feelings toward them and how much respect she will give or demand of them. I have been extremely blessed to have a wonderful and caring father who treated me like I was special. Maybe being the first girl after the birth of seven boys had something to do with it.

Our relationship is very precious and difficult to describe. It is a lifelong bond cemented in respect for all that is sacred and blessed. My father gave me many gifts, but the greatest gift he gave me was instilling spiritual values in me at a very early age. Even though he was the head of our household and a giant of a man, he looked to a higher force. He taught me to have faith in God and to love God with all my heart, soul, and mind. He taught me how to worship and about the power of prayer and the importance of the word of God. He was stern but fair, strict but forgiving, and always loving.

My father also happens to be one of the funniest men I know. "A cheerful heart doeth good like a medicine..." (Proverbs 17:22) is another lesson I learned from him. It is because of my father and my mother's teachings and their living example that I have escaped many of life's storms. Even now if I need advice or guidance, I call them because I know they will have Godly wisdom. They have never led me down the wrong path.

I grew up knowing I was loved, protected, and respected by my father; therefore, I loved and respected him. To this very day I use the knowledge my father gave me to help pattern the lives of my children, so that they will have the courage to live healthy and productive lives. And I have a great husband who loves, protects, and respects me. I, with joy, love and respect him in return.

My father is indeed one of the main reasons I live a happy and fulfilled life. For this, I will always love you. Thanks, Dad!

"I Have to Let Them Go"

It scared the heck out of me when my wife said she wanted to have children, because in medical school all I saw were the things that could go wrong in pregnancy and birth and delivery. When we had our first daughter, Bree, I felt we rolled the dice and got lucky. I didn't want to do it again—I didn't think we should push our luck— but we were blessed with another healthy girl, Erin.

I always thought when I was younger that I could do a better job than my parents did, that I would never make their mistakes with my children. Looking back, I realize my father raised me well. He drove me hard to be the best at whatever I chose to do, and he taught me the importance of family. I've tried to pass these lessons on to my children while adding a third: tolerance and acceptance of others.

There are definitely things I think I've done better than my parents, and there are things I don't think I've done well. I've tried to be a good teacher, but my children have said I have no patience when I teach them, and that drives me nuts. When they were younger and would bring their homework to me, I would try to approach math problems or science problems from a lot of different angles. I thought I was showing tremendous patience. Evidently I wasn't.

Where I've succeeded, I think, is in teaching them caution, responsibility, and the bigger picture of life: That the 'A' on the test means nothing—it's what you learn. That this person just did something to hurt you, but why? Is it because he's spiteful and mean or because he's insecure? I think I've taught them to dig deeper into what they see and not always take things at face value.

There's a word in the Yiddish language: _nachas_. It means happiness: those really good experiences you hold dear to your heart. It's the excitement I feel when I see life through their eyes, when I feel their exuberance and remember my life and growing up and what youth is supposed to be.

Some of the best times are when they come home and they've learned something. Bree was telling me the other day that she saw a documentary on the JFK assassination and she said, "No way was there a single assassin." It was a huge revelation for her, because it was the first time she was beginning to think, "Maybe I'm getting false or incomplete information." She begins the questioning part of her life now. It's neat to see that.

Erin likes to play soccer and run track, and when she scores a goal or wins a race and comes home with a special grade, with that beaming smile, that's _nachas_.

As my girls become independent and approach the time they'll leave home, a fear I had before they were born is resurfacing. Recently they both got cars, and every time they go out I have these anxieties I don't speak of. I tell my Erin that if she kills herself, I'm going to hurt her bad.

This is a really important time for them, a thrilling time. This is a time when you catch the comet and ride. I'm so excited, vicariously, for them. I'm also concerned about whether they have all the tools they need. I just don't know. But it's time, so I have to let them go.

Bree Danielle

When my sister and I were little, my dad would buy a new mask every year to scare us with. He would chase us around the house and we would laugh. As we have grown up, the laughter has turned to, "Dad, it's not funny!" but he still pursues the giggle. Even though his jokes have become a little stale, I would never want them to end. I've grown attached to his silly behavior and constant struggle to make Erin and me react.

I was going through my baby book the other day and I found a letter from the Tooth Fairy, otherwise known as my dad. He wrote that my sister had woken up while he was taking my tooth to the "Hall of Fame" and that he had to sprinkle fairy dust on her nose. Reading the letter, specifically that phrase, made me laugh. I realized how hard he had tried, whether it was to make us laugh or to make us understand. Well, Dad, after seventeen years of lame jokes and scary masks, you occupy a huge space in our hearts. Thank you for the smiles.

Great Man   *Erin*

A man who fights everyday against disease and oppression
Who searches for the good in all mankind
Who loves someone not by their appearance, but
by his heart and determination.
Who can be the best cook, doctor, and dad all at
once and still rescue you from the big bad wolves at night.
Who loves his children as if they were the world and
would climb to the ends of the earth to save them.
We are his universe and he is my knight in shining armor.
The Great Man in my life is my superman, my dad.

HOWIE MANDEL *Father /* | **RILEY** *Son*
Actor / Comedian | **ALEX** *Daughter*
| **JACKIE** *Daughter*

"I Can't Believe I'm Someone's Dad"

Every day I get up and think to myself, "I can't believe I'm someone's dad." My biggest fear is that my kids are thinking the same thing. I always wanted children but found the concept overwhelming. I remember thinking, "How can I possibly teach a child anything?" From the moment I witnessed the miracle of the birth of my first child, I became a different person. The teaching began. As it turns out, I am the student. My children teach me love, responsibility, priorities, and pretty much every lesson in life. They are my life. They are all that matters. But I still can't believe I'm someone's dad!

KATHY IRELAND *Daughter /*
Model / Actor

JOHN IRELAND *Father /*
Retired Labor Union Representative

CYNTHIA *Daughter*

MARY *Daughter*

"The Richest Family in the World"

On my fifth birthday, I successfully blew out all the candles, only to have them re-light. I opened a heavy, brick-shaped birthday present, and there was a brick inside. I didn't know what to think. Then my dad started laughing. When he laughs, his whole body shakes, especially his face, but sound doesn't really come out. He finally gave me my real present, a pickup truck that I could sit on and make go by scooting my feet, and I got the joke. He was always a huge practical joker—April Fool's Day was always a big event in our house.

As a little girl, I remember thinking that my mom was so lucky to have found my dad, and I worried that I would never find anyone who compared to him. My dad helped the little guy, the underdog, as a retail clerks' union representative. If people were not being treated fairly, Dad would fight for them. I remember baking cookies with my mom for the families of strikers, marching with my dad in picket lines, and attending a Cesar Chavez rally. Dad would take us to Tijuana, Mexico, and show us cardboard houses that so many families had to live in.

At dinner when Dad would pray, he would say, "Thank you, God, for making me the richest man in the world." We had everything we needed, so I assumed he was talking about money. I didn't realize he was talking about his family. My parents had financial difficulties, but I always felt in every respect that we were the richest family in the world. Dad taught us to appreciate the beauty that God created. Everything fun that we did was free. My childhood is filled with memories of hiking, camping, fishing, going to the beach, and collecting shells and rocks.

Dad taught me the importance of knowing how to take care of myself. When I was a kid, if I wanted money, Dad would suggest ways for me to earn it. I did extra chores, painted rocks and sold them door to door, washed people's cars, sold lemonade and vegetables from our garden. When I was 11, I got my first serious job delivering newspapers. On Sunday mornings, Dad got up at 5:30 a.m. and helped me fold papers. He always told me to do more than what is expected of me: If people expect the newspaper to land on the driveway, he'd say, put it on the front porch. I was awarded Carrier of the Year for my district all three years I had the route.

The things Dad taught me as a child and continues to teach me have a major impact on my life today. In all of my business dealings, I think of my dad and how he fought for people to be treated fairly. Dad taught me the importance of being a good worker, and he told me I could be anything I wanted to be—I could be the first woman President if I wanted to. I always believed him and I still do. The confidence I gained from knowing Dad believed in me led me never to compromise myself. I have walked off jobs in bad situations. I've always known I could do anything else for a living.

All my life, my dad has told me that he loves me, and he has given me lots of hugs and love and respect. I think I took that for granted and assumed all dads were that way. Now that I'm older, I realize how rare and precious that love is. We were, indeed, the richest family in the world.

"Never Too Old to Hold Your Hand"

My sons, you have made me the proudest father in the world. I thank God for the day you were born.

My oldest, Husain: You have grown into a caring, loving, and responsible young man. I was so proud at your college graduation, yet saddened by the fact that you were leaving home to start your own life. I'm always here for you. Remember, I love you.

My youngest, Juaquin: Jake, to learn you were blind at birth saddened me, but to see you accomplish so much in your short life pleases me. Your poetry and public speaking bring me so much joy. Your willingness to face each challenge head on gives me the strength to face my own challenges. You'll always have my love and support.

Husain

Dad, you represent love, strength, and family. You have never hesitated to show your feelings. You have kept going forward regardless of your pains and struggles. You have always worked hard at providing for us and have always been there for us when we needed you. You've taught me what it takes to grow into a man. When I get married and have a family, these are the qualities I want to pass on to my children.

Juaquin "Jake"

Dad, you've done whatever it takes for me to have the best that life can offer. You've sacrificed so many of your own dreams, but you have never stopped to complain. Instead, you keep on making things better for me. I would never have come this far in my life if it weren't for you, Dad. You have never made a decision or choice without considering what effect it will have on my education, health, and life. Dad, you're my hero.

Our Dad

As we each grow to become a young man
We're never too old to hold your hand.

You're that special spark in our lives
That goes on burning and will never die.

Dad, you'll never disappear from our hearts.
You're the one we love, in all of our thoughts.

We love you, DAD!!

DAVID KEITH *Son / Actor* | **LEM KEITH** *Father*

"Gifts"

Gifts from my father
Pulling for the underdog
Big Band music
Unfettered imagination
Hatred of racism
Democratic Party
Methodist Church
Barbershop harmony
Tennessee Volunteers
The Jitterbug
Love of God
Eye for the ladies
My mother
My sister
Talent
Pursuit of perfection
Relentless support
Undying love

"Come Pick Up Your Boys"

Adoption: What a unique way to become a father!

My wife and I had tried in vitro fertilization several times unsuccessfully, and we finally got to the point where we felt like the thing to do was to adopt. We have such a special marriage, and there was so much love in our hearts that we just knew we were meant to be parents. I don't remember this—my wife had to remind me later—but when we first began the adoption process, the counselor asked us whether we would be interested in twins, and I said I thought that would be really something. She especially liked to remind me of that at three in the morning, when we were up with both of them.

But we never dreamed that there would be two! When we knew our baby was coming, we went through the usual steps of buying all the equipment. Then we got a call from the agency, saying, "You can come pick up your boys." This was a complete surprise to us! So we did what we had to do: We went shopping again.

Brian and Rusty came to us when they were four days old, and it has been a love affair ever since. They have so filled my life with love, affection, and activity that it is hard to remember what it was like before they arrived. The greatest challenge for us is that they're two completely different people. They have different interests, different sensibilities and personalities, and we constantly have to be aware of that and to help each one find the road that's right for him.

It's very clear to me that God has special plans for them, and I am grateful to have been given the awesome responsibility of molding and shaping them for whatever lies ahead. Nothing makes me prouder than to overhear one of them tell someone nearby, "That's my dad!"

"The Letter"

My life now is so abundant, so bursting with happiness—a husband and children who are at the center of a rich existence blessed beyond belief. It was a struggle to get here though, and along the way I called upon my daddy to guide me. In my father's eyes I was always something special—dancing alternately between princess and powerhouse.

In my mind, Daddy could do anything. Other little girls loved to go to ride the ponies with their daddies, but I loved nothing more than going to Daddy's office. The first one I could remember held a principal's desk, and I could barely see over it. Much later his office would be an executive suite and Daddy was into politics. The massive mahogany desk held a world of mystery for me as lights from phone lines blinked with the urgency of untold opportunities. Being with him gave me a sense of ambition—I wanted to be important like Daddy.

I grew up in South Carolina at a time when integration was still a social experiment and my dad was a civil rights leader. I watched him give speeches and call for racial harmony and opportunity for all. I saw him make unpopular decisions against popular people, and I learned the power of conviction.

Our house was never one of those "wait until your father gets home" type of households—Mom had her own power, and Daddy always respected that. No matter how mad I got with my mother, Dad would never say an unsupportive, unkind word about her. They had their disagreements, but he defended her point of view in public and in private. From him I learned devotion.

As serious as Dad was about his work, he was also serious about his play. A world-class cutup, Daddy could tell jokes better than anyone I knew—jokes that would go on for an eternity before the punch line. It was one of the things we shared—a storyteller's glib tendency to exaggerate and embellish any little thread of a tale to get more power in the end. Dad, my brother, and I would tell jokes while Mom would roll her eyes in mock exasperation. I felt like one of the boys, and I got my first rush of being in the spotlight. I loved his humor and could see it covered a lot of pain—from him, I learned to laugh.

I often wonder what dreams Daddy had to jettison in favor of providing for a family and securing a future. The stoic side of him doesn't allow him to share those disappointments, but when my first child was born we were all together as a family, and Daddy stood to make a toast. We expected him to be humorous and brief so we could dig into the marvelous meal Mom had made, but Daddy got something caught in his throat— something a sip of wine wouldn't clear. It was far too strong to suppress, and years of hopes and wishing-upon-stars and prayers to God came flooding out. He could see his legacy unfolding, and it was overwhelming to him. His grandchildren held the promise of all the things undone in his life—from him, I learned hopefulness.

I have never told Daddy what I cherish most about being his daughter and what essence of him I try to pass along to my children. It is his sense of being alive that has always resonated with me, the fact that he's always striving and reaching, yet somehow happy with this precise moment in time. He had an ability to have great expectations of me while also offering great acceptance. His rule was, "Go out there and take it—the future is yours. Make it happen. Don't be afraid to fail. You won't, but if you do, you can always come home."

A father's love is an anchor in our lives like a strong shoulder to lean on. After I left home I never thought I would need that kind of strength and support from Daddy, but then I never thought I would be divorced, either. It seems so distant now, but at the time the pain came crashing in from all sides, including that voice in me that cried out about disappointing Daddy. He flew across the country to be with me, and in case I ever doubted it, he wrote these words to me in a letter that I keep close to my heart. It says more than I ever could about who my father is.

Dear Leeza,

Leeza, I know there's nothing I can do to ease the stress you're under right now. I do want you to know how very much we all love you, and when the world seems to be caving in on your shoulders, please know you can always call and we will help you hold it up, even if we can't help you put it down.

Life is wonderfully strange and bizarre, yet it is simple and common. The "ups" and "downs" seem to keep coming as the rolling peaks and valleys on a mountain chain. The precipices are fabulous, and the valleys are the pits. Unfortunately, we have to experience both of these in life—without failure how would we know success and without success how would we know failure?

Remember, success is getting up just one more time than you fall, and there's not a tumble in this world that can keep you down. You're an incredibly strong person and errors of the heart will always be rectified by your intellectual honesty and integrity. Your caring, compassion, and desire to be fair beyond a shadow may have caused your grief, but even this may be more desirable than to lose the joy that caring can bring.

Leeza, I feel some fatherly guilt in your frustrations at this juncture in your life. Perhaps I could have helped you to be more aware. Perhaps I could have set a better father-daughter example for you. Perhaps I could have instilled a resilience in you for detecting flaws in character, morality, or ethics. I take a portion of your sorrows and regrets as my own.

Your drive for excellence and strong sense of commitment are admirable traits. There can be no progress without a degree of adventure into the unknown. Your willingness to probe the mind and the heart for meaning will ultimately bring you unparalleled peace, joy, and security.

Leeza, I would hope you do not grow tired, hostile, or hopeless in your search for a higher meaning in your life. I don't know why I would even suppose you would be unable to handle the situation you find yourself in at present. Even as a child growing up, sometimes in a mixed emotional environment, you showed the stamina and leadership qualities that have served you well. Do not fear, these traits will not desert you in this hour of challenge.

"I Believe in Being Around"

Going out to eat, running into the bookstore, cruising the record store for music we both enjoy, planning a family vacation to an amusement park with a dozen roller coasters, enduring father-daughter driving lessons, attending volleyball games: There's no such thing as a typical day with a teenager.

I don't believe in scheduling an hour and a half and making sure you're busy and bonding and all those other buzzwords. I believe in being around. Maybe it's because my father wasn't around so much when I was young. He was an insurance salesman, and up until I was about thirteen, he traveled every week. I didn't miss the time with him because I didn't know any better. When you're a kid, that's just life. But I've consciously tried to spend more time with my daughter, and my business has allowed me to do that.

To my dad's credit, he was there for me when I most needed him. After I was injured in an industrial accident about twenty years ago, I went to be with my parents for my rehabilitation. My dad built an above-ground swimming pool in the back yard so I could swim laps. Later on, he put up a building around it so it wouldn't be cold in the winter. We were always building little gadgets or contraptions to help with my rehabilitation or to help me do things. He was instrumental in helping me come back from my accident.

I don't know if Amy looks upon things differently because of my situation. She's pretty quiet, kind of like me, and I've never asked her. I have always been this way to her. Sometimes, because my hands were burned in the accident, I'll get her to help me when I can't open the brand new jar of jelly or get a nut started on a bolt. I don't ask often.

Now that Amy's a teenager, she doesn't want to be around her parents as much, but we're there for her. I've tried to be supportive when she's disappointed about something, to take care of her when she's sick, to help her over the bumps in life. In the teenage years, sometimes it seems every day is a bump. But I'm around for all of them, for her.

ALFRED McEWEN *Father / Baritone*

BILLY *Son*

KAREN *Daughter*

MARK *Son / CBS This Morning Anchor*

LESLIE *Daughter*

SEAN *Son*

CHRISTOPHER *Son*

"The Greatest Role of My Life"

My dad died when I was five months old, so being a daddy to my own children was always important to me. They are the most important treasures my wife and I possess.

Billy, you have had a love affair with automobiles since you were three, swinging your red kiddie-car in and out of other kiddie-car traffic the same way Daddy did with his single-seat Plymouth. You still love to drive and travel. I love to listen to your stories about the people you meet and the places you see as a long-distance tour bus operator. Whenever I need assistance around the old place, you either know how to repair it or where help can be obtained. You have been a rock to me.

Leslie, my Sessie, you and I hit it off from the very beginning. We read, sang, went to the movies. You didn't want to share my attention. Once, when I noticed baby Mark was about to cry, I saw you were pinching him to get him away from the spot you deemed yours, next to me. I was overwhelmed by your affection, and it has never faltered all of your wonderful life. What a pleasant shock to learn you were so vocally talented. I still love singing with my baby.

Mark, I used to look at you and wonder what you would become. You were a whiz with language and a fine athlete. Before I knew it, you were off to make your fortune in California. The rest is beautiful history. I was proud to see you named one of the most respected television personalities. You have always been kind and generous with your colleagues and your family. I am deeply grateful for the sustained support you have provided your autistic brother and his organization, Community Services for Autistic Adults and Children. Thank you for sharing so much of your magical life with us all.

Karen, I will never forget the night of your birth. It was Christmas Eve. Your mother and I were choir director and organist for a little military chapel in Zweibrucken, Germany. You arrived right after we finished the service with a mad dash to the military hospital. What a beautiful baby! We spoiled you rotten. Then came the moment of magic when you were the first of our children to become a parent. I am so proud of the wife, mom, and homemaker you have become.

Beloved Sean, you amazed us with the difference in development and attitude you showed as you grew. Our German friends thought you were such a good child because you never cried, except for food. No interacting with us, no recognition of Mom or Dad. I knew something had to be wrong. After reading everything I could get my hands on, I knew you were autistic, but I could not find a soul to support my conclusions. When a retired Army doctor confirmed it, I cried with relief, and we began searching for a way to deal with the awful malady. With the help of CSAAC, you are working and living in a beautiful atmosphere.

Christopher—the Kirkster—you always seemed to know what you wanted to do with your life. You were a bright child and excelled throughout school. I'm proud of your work as a radio personality and thankful for your love and support in all my undertakings. Through you, I've met the governor and other big wigs. You've had me on your radio show to sing jazz. You have been supportive of Sean and his organization.

What a great bunch of children God gave us! With their spouses and children, we have a beautiful extended family. We support each other. We like being together. We fuss a little, but we hug a lot. Being a daddy is the greatest role of my life.

"Accomplishing Our Goals"

I think I got my work ethic from my dad. My mom's more laid back, but my dad works hard and loves what he does. The same with me. We both like the self-satisfaction you get when you accomplish your goal—his with a patient, mine in competition. We're both really organized. We like things clean. We make lists and like to get everything done. I guess we're kind of high-strung people. My dad used to tell me stories before I'd go to bed, and he's the only dad I know who would quiz you after to make sure you were listening.

I spent a lot of time away from home because of gymnastics. It was definitely hard on me, but at the same time, I think it made me grow up and appreciate my parents that much more. My dad devoted all his time off to visiting me or seeing competitions. When I was at home, my dad put in really long, hard hours, and so did I—going to school and that sort of thing. So in some ways I saw him more when I lived away from home, because when he came to visit me, he couldn't work or do anything else. He was with me.

When it comes to my dad—and my mom too—I'm not like a typical nineteen-year-old. I really like being with my parents. I realize you can't take them for granted. Being away from home so much, I realized that family is the most important thing, because when things are going well everyone likes you, but it's your parents who help you through all the hard times.

Burt Strug:

Keri is my baby. The other kids were raised when I was in cardiac surgery residency and I was gone most of the time. When Keri was born, I was in private practice and had scheduled time off to be with the family. My relationship with Keri is based on mutual respect for each other's goals and commitments outside the family. When Keri became devoted to gymnastics, we talked about love, trust, and being there. She came to me for encouragement and help in coping with her ups and downs. I came to her for quality time, for youth, for a change of scenery, and for a vicarious thrill of experiencing her unique childhood. Keri never really had a childhood. She went from being a little girl to being a driven, dedicated world-class athlete.

Our philosophy of a positive approach to all our efforts gave both of us the courage and internal energy to keep on trying to excel. With every injury Keri endured, I would tell her about myself and other people—how you can achieve whatever you want if you really try hard. Keri's work ethic is unbelievable. Her mental and physical energy to achieve success was constantly demonstrated in everything she did in and out of the gym.

I do not think Keri realized that I leaned on her as much as she leaned on me. Neither one of us ever wanted to disappoint the other, and we would go to great lengths to live up to each other's expectations. I think being away from each other since she was thirteen-years-old made us more conscious and aware of the need to be supportive. We never took each other for granted.

If parents live vicariously through their children, then I have been very close to heaven.

BHAVYEN SANGHAVI *Father /* | **SUMANT** *Grandfather*
Chemical Engineer | **POOJA** *Daughter*
| **NUPAR** *Daughter*

"Hope for the Future"

The way it was!

With fulfillment comes responsibility,

Short-term memory,

Hope for the future,

No hope on a rope,

Runny nose,

Ceaseless noise,

Unlimited energy,

Sweet insanity,

Gentle but firm,

But, Dad, everyone at school is wearing them,

To the poorhouse with a smile,

Wash your hands,

Chocolate cake for breakfast,

Love, wisdom, and then freedom,

She's got the whole world in her hands,

Each a gift of pleasure and love,

In my daughters, Pooja and Nupar, I see all of life.

JON HANSON *Father /*
Professor of Law, Harvard University

ERIN *Daughter*
EMILY *Daughter*

"A Love Letter to My Children"

Dear Emily and Erin (and your future siblings, if any),

After accepting your Uncle Bill's invitation to contribute something to his book, I decided to write you a letter, which, like a time capsule launched into space or a bottled message thrown into the outgoing tide, may never be discovered by its intended recipients. If you do come across this someday, I hope it will give you some strength and perspective.

I write this in the wake of a significant moment in my career: One month ago I was voted tenure by the faculty of the Harvard Law School. Before you were born, such a milestone would have figured as prominently as any other on my life's landscape. But today career ambitions seem distant and overshadowed by the two curious and energetic souls who dominate my life and the life of Kathleen, their wonderful mother.

Emily, you are four-years-old—or, as you insist, "four and three quarters." Erin, eight weeks ago you turned one—still too young to utter, "one and one sixth," and too innocent to recognize the status implications of those two extra months.

When Uncle Bill told me the title of his book, I initially planned to write about the ways I shouldered your burdens. But then it occurred to me that I had it backward. My shoulders are so far largely untested. They have served only to ease the pain of some ill-fated toddles and to assuage the fears and frustrations of a bright and sensitive preschooler. Yet on your tiny shoulders, I lean every day.

Of course, I do not lean in the literal sense that, say, Danny's father does in Roald Dahl's book, *Danny the Champion of the World*. In that tale—one of Emily's favorites—young Danny rescues his father from a pit and then serves as a human crutch as his father holds tight to Danny's shoulders and struggles to walk with one badly injured leg. As he leads his ailing father to safety, Danny urges, "Go on, Dad...you can lean harder than that."

On your shoulders, I lean figuratively, but lean nonetheless and to much the same effect. Lest my memories be eclipsed by next year's traumas and triumphs, let me briefly describe my impressions of each of you at this moment and, in the process, reveal a few of the hundreds of ways in which you support me.

Erin, you are best known at this age for being fearless and sweet. But you are also affectionate—ever eager to hug and kiss us—and you love to make us laugh. And sometimes you are a quiet, even contemplative, observer. As I sit with you in our backyard sandbox and watch you play with and marvel at the intractable and dynamic sand formations and the black ants and green caterpillars that happen by, I witness your seemingly insatiable appetite for touching, holding, and understanding the mundane objects around us. To you, they are new and mysterious. I hear your steady, soft breathing, think of your fresh eyes, and begin to see the world through them myself. Because of you I can sometimes glimpse with wonder the extraordinary opportunity that we're each given to experience a piece of this amazing universe. As I watch you deliberately lifting the sand-filled plastic garden shovel to your mouth for a taste, I am reminded of a line by thirteenth century Islamic poet and mystic Jelaluddin Rumi. "There are hundreds of ways to kneel and kiss the ground." Thank you, Erin, for your kisses.

Emily, you are loving, sensitive, funny, and smart. And just like your younger sister, and despite my admonitions, you are growing up too fast. Nurse Brown announced last week that your forty inches place you in the 95th percentile among five-year-old girls. It's really not your physical height that startles your six-foot, five-inch father. From my vantage point, you still appear to be a tiny child. Rather, it's your non-physical stature that sometimes overwhelms me. Three fleeting years ago, you toddled through life as Erin now does. One year ago, you spent most days in costume, pretending to be one or another character—Batman or Cinderella or Captain Hook or the Wicked Witch of the East or Matilda or Luke Skywalker or Little Bear. You sometimes changed outfits four times in a day. With every switch, your mother and I were required to play the role of your character's counterparts. The characters rarely visit these days. When I ask about them or invite one to join us, you explain, "Pretending is for little kids." At such moments, I feel as though I'm standing on a dock, watching a lover sailing away on a long journey. "Will you return? Who will you be when you come back? I will miss you."

When, in the next moment, a taller, faster boat returns to the dock I marvel at the strong, generous, loving "big kid" who steps off. Emily, your mother and I could not have wished for a better big sister for Erin. In the countless times over the past year that Erin has torn apart the puzzle you were working on, grabbed the toy that you were playing with, or otherwise occupied the space in the household that was once yours, you have met her with a smile, often a laugh, and a reassuring, "It's okay. She can have it."

At the end of most days, just before bedtime, the pair of you pull your Mom and me out onto the living room floor to dance to your favorite song. Kate and Anna McGarrigle sing about racing to catch a boat that will get them to the other side, while you both do your best to dance to the locomotive beat and to sing:

> Sixty minutes sixty miles
>
> Thirty minutes thirty miles
>
> Twenty minutes twenty miles
>
> Ten nine eight
>
> But I could not slow down
>
> No, I could not slow down.

When either of you grows weary of dancing, you raise your arms to me, and I happily take my cue to pick you up and hold you close. Swaying back and forth and feeling your breath on my neck, I wonder who is leaning on whom, and I wish a secret wish that you could somehow slow down.

If and when you read this letter, I expect you will be growing, or will have already grown, into intelligent and independent young adults. As independent as you may be, there will be occasions when you need love, support, advice, or just someone to dance with. Please come to us. Your mother and I have strong shoulders. And we owe you. As big as you may believe your burden to be, bring it to us.

Go on, my darlings. You can lean harder than that.

"The Finest Man I've Ever Known"

Dear Daddy,

Today and every day, I am thankful that you are my father. Spoken or unspoken, I have always known that you love me. You have taught me to be brave and strong, tender and kind, giving and forgiving. When I was a little girl, I thought you were magic and you hung the moon. Now that I'm a big girl, I know you are, and you do! My life has taken me on such a wonderful journey. Because of the confidence that you instilled in me, I have the courage to travel through life.

You will probably never know what a great and rare man you are, and that is part of what makes you special. I don't always do what's right, but I know what's right because of you. You'd say you were just doing what a father does. I'd say you're the finest man I've ever known.

I thank God every day that you're my daddy. I love you.

"True Happiness"

"There is a time for everything, and a season for every activity under the heavens."

My life has been filled with the pursuit of happiness, which over the years has come in a variety of forms. As a child, it was making my dear departed mother happy by behaving well. Later, as a teen, happiness was the pursuit of being a standout student and athlete. When that pursuit carried me through college and into the NFL, for years I felt there could be nothing greater. I was a professional football player, making a great living, and having the time of my life. I was in control of my world. But as the verse states, that chapter of my life came to an end. I again began the quest to find that special something or someone who could make me happy.

When I met Lisa, now my wife of seven years, happiness was again within my reach. She gave my life meaning. She was someone I so dearly needed, someone to love. Life, I felt again, was complete. But three years later, I would be blessed with the greatest gift of all—the birth of our first son, Hayden Colby Graham. What a miracle! At first sight of Hayden, my whole view of life and the true meaning of happiness changed. Never before had I felt the joy that came from holding him in my arms. That night, I fell in love with his presence. Nothing, I thought, could ever give me such happiness again—until three years later, when my second son was born. Gavin Cole Graham was a second gift from God.

What a wonderful feeling that God would grant me the privilege to share my love with not one but two wonderful babies. I look forward to each day and the years to come with my sons, for it is with them that I have discovered true happiness.

"A Long Walk Together"

Dear Trey and Charley,

The simple word "Dad" from your lips can elicit the strongest emotions from me. I am constantly amazed at how easily I am hurt by your innocent anger and then healed by your unselfish love—all in the same few precious breaths. But most of all I feel totally blessed to be the one person in the world that you call "Dad."

Trey-bird, you were our first miracle baby. My spinal cord injury was supposed to prevent your natural birth, but on Christmas Eve 1987, you came to us wrapped in God's love. It was a gift that would make the Christmas season more special forever. You are a sensitive, loving human being. I will always admire your tenacity, and I beam with pride as you excel in sports. You are blessed with athletic talent, but you also can be a winner in the classroom. You are an inquisitive, imaginative young man, and you have a zest for learning.

Charley, my boy, you were our second miracle baby, and what a perfect second son you are. Almost a Halloween baby, you are definitely our special treat—although you also excel in tricks! For all the good qualities you share with Trey, you are also unique in your own right. Your confidence and athletic ability are boundless. Your mind is as quick as your feet, and I am so proud of your commitment to learning.

Boys, your old dad is very sentimental. There are many times when I am away that I find myself tearing up just thinking of you. You are my motivation to succeed. God truly blessed your birth, and I pray that I can be as good a father to you as Paw Paw is to me. I have such a wonderful father-son relationship and, if I can even come close to sharing that level of love with you, then I'll have provided you with strong values for life.

I do want so badly to share your sports with you. I wanted to be the one who taught you how to throw and how to catch, how to dribble and how to swim, how to fish and how to ski. I am so thankful that you understand. I will always be here for advice, support, and encouragement. I will always be your most faithful fan.

And, God willing, you and I will one day take a long walk together and leave this wheelchair behind. I love you.

Dad

Once Upon a Time...
there was a little old man
who used to spend his entire day walking along the beach.
The beach was cluttered with starfish
and the old man worked hard at throwing them back into the ocean,
with the hope that they wouldn't suffocate and die.
One day a young man approached the elderly man and said,
"Old man, I watch you walk this beach day in and day out,
hours at a time, nearly every day of the week.
What are you doing?"
The old man explained to the younger man how the starfish would
suffocate and die if he didn't throw them back into the water.
The younger man said,
"But old man, this beach is covered with starfish!
There's no way you can make a difference!"
To that, the old man simply bent down, picked up a starfish,
and threw it back into the ocean, and then said,
"For that one, I just did."

TRAVIS TRITT *Son /* **JAMES TRITT** *Father*

Recording Artist

"Seeing Him in Me"

Being my dad's son was never easy. Because of his high expectations and his impatience with me, I often felt I had failed him. It was not until I became a man that I came to appreciate him for who he is and all that he taught me.

A good provider and a hard worker, he showed me that you appreciate something you work for much more than something that is handed to you. I hope I can provide for my family as well as he has for his.

He taught me to stand up for what I believe in, even when it's unpopular. I've found the criticism this brings in the short term is well worth the respect it commands in the long run. My dad is proud to be known as a man who speaks his mind. I share that label and that pride.

My dad is a man you can count on. No matter what the circumstances, if he starts a job, you can bet he will finish it. That sheer determination and will is a survival skill that I draw on daily.

His simple "country boy business sense" could rival that of many New York corporate executives. Whether it is buying a used car or selling a piece of property, he always makes the deal work in his favor. I try to follow his example in my own business affairs.

My dad has a sincere love for the simple beauty of nature. He has always had a tremendous appreciation for a piece of land that lay just right or a rippling creek with a waterfall that has cascaded over the same smooth rocks for hundreds of years. I share his love for the great outdoors.

My dad taught me to respect history and tradition. Like him, I'm drawn to old things—farm equipment, barns, handmade guitars, guns, knives, furniture—that show a craftsmanship that's rare today.

We also share a love of motorcycles. In 1990, I bought a Harley-Davidson with my first record royalty check and invited my dad on a road trip that included a drive through the Great Smoky Mountains. We bonded as a father and son on that trip more than we ever had. A Paul Overstreet song says it best:

> "I'm seeing my father in me.
> I guess that's how it's meant to be.
> And I find I'm more and more like him each day.
> I notice I walk the way he walks.
> I notice I talk the way he talks.
> Yes, I'm starting to see my father in me."

I give him credit for much of what I am. I will always be proud to be his son.

"Good with Growing Things"

My dad is good with growing things: flowers, plants, trees, and children. You can pick out my parents' house from the street by the beautiful landscaping and gorgeous flowers. Inside, you can tell it's my dad's home because it reflects his quiet strength, warmth, and love.

When I first started doing a lot of modeling and acting, my mother was the one who was with me, but my dad was the main person in the household, raising my two brothers and working a full-time job to pay the bills. He probably worked twice as hard just to keep everything together.

Today, when I'm off working somewhere, I can call my dad up and he'll take time off from his job to fly up and visit me. It's a big deal because he hates to fly, but he never complains because he wants to see me and make sure I'm okay. Anytime I get to travel to someplace really beautiful, I love to bring him.

My dad is a shy, reserved man, but you can see how he cares about people through what he does. Ultimately, I think a lot of people can say things and not "do." I think he knows the most important thing is what you do for somebody and not what you say for somebody.

When I get married, the man I choose will be a lot like my father, because he's everything that I could ever want in somebody as a life partner: gentle, hardworking, and loving. I would want my husband to be that way with my children—good with growing things.

"Loathing the Demons"

My greatest joy and my greatest regret are both associated with my five children and their ten children. The joy flows from the endless satisfaction, pride, hope, and pleasure that go with being a father and a grandfather. It is beyond my capacity to imagine what my life would have been without the delights of being a father. My chief regret is that for too many years my career and personal interests claimed too many of the hours that should have been shared with my young family. This was a loss not only to them but also to me.

Fortunately, since leaving the U.S. Senate in 1981, I have increasingly seized on the opportunities to share more time and participate in the lives of my children and grandchildren. It has helped me appreciate that there is life in abundance beyond the still-challenging world of politics.

At Christmastime 1994, my wife, Eleanor and I were given the sad news at midnight that our third daughter, Teresa Jane, had been found frozen to death in the snows of Wisconsin after falling because of intoxication. She was a delightful, intelligent, humorous young woman who had struggled for years to overcome alcoholism. When she died, I could scarcely carry the burden of sorrow and regret that seized my every waking hour and troubled sleep.

Terry's death has painfully brought to my heart and mind just how precious and fragile are the lives of those we love. Paradoxically, her presence has never been more real to me than in these days since her death. Beyond this, I feel a new sense of appreciation and love for my children who survive—and indeed, my compassion and love for all human beings have deepened as I have struggled to come to terms with the loss of dear Terry.

Terry's tragic and losing struggle to overcome her addiction to alcohol has dramatized for me the necessity of separating our loathing, as parents, of the demons that sometimes afflict our children from our love of the children victimized by these demons.

Every human being longs to be loved and needs to be loved—especially those who suffer from dreaded diseases such as alcoholism and its frequent companion—depression—both of which afflicted Terry.

Loving Terry and mourning her death have, I believe, made me a more caring and compassionate father.

CHERYL LADD *Daughter/ Actor*

MARION "STOPPY" STOPPELMOOR *Father*

"My Hero"

I watched as she expertly brushed the lipstick over her mouth. She glanced down, winked at me, and smiled that conspiratorial "this is our special day, isn't it wonderful?" smile. I felt overwhelmed by how much she loved me and how willing she was to share her happiness and excitement. I was six years old, and I knew my mother was beautiful.

"Let's go, sweetie," she said. "We don't want to be late."

Off we dashed, my mother, my older sister Mary Ann, and me. We were about to do something we had done many times before, something we would cherish forever.

It took a mere seven minutes to arrive at our destination. Mary Ann and I raced from the car, already singing at the top of our lungs. We ran straight to the platform, which imagination had long ago transformed into a Broadway stage. As we continued our song and dance we glanced up and down the deserted track and gazed across the vast prairie, which was turning to gold in the late afternoon light. The anticipation and excitement were building with each chorus. We were high-kicking and belting it out to a captive audience of railroad ties and tumbleweeds.

At exactly the same instant we stopped and looked at each other. We stood dead still and listened. Silence! Our hearts were beating like hummingbirds' wings from the exertion of our command performance and the knowledge of what was near. We held hands and held our breath. Then we heard it!

A deep, piercing whistle blew across the plain. Quietly at first, then steadily building, the rhythmic chug-a-chug of the steel wheels on the tracks reached our ears.

"It's him. He's coming!" I hollered.

I looked over my shoulder for my mother, but she had heard it too and was walking eagerly toward us.

The sound grew louder and louder as it rushed closer and closer. The machine looked huge and fierce, almost alive. At that exact moment, when the immense beast was slowing down, almost upon us, and my awe was turning into fear, an arm appeared through its small window and a familiar hand waved from high in the air.

As the train shuddered to a stop, the handsome blond man looked down at us and grinned from ear to ear. Without a word, he leapt from the cab and bounded toward us, arms outstretched. He gathered up his three little women and wrapped us in his strong and loving arms.

Daddy was home. All was right with the world.

I love you, Dad. You are my hero, and you always will be!

JOHN T. SKELLY *Father /*
Retired White House Correspondent

RITA *Daughter*

PATTIE *Daughter*

BETH *Daughter*

JOHN *Son*

ANNIE *Daughter*

Father's Day just passed, and the cards came in as usual:

"You have mended my broken toys, my broken dreams, and put them all back together with love, patience, and understanding."

My four charming daughters got their looks and sweet soul from their mother. I met her in September 1952, going through the cafeteria line at George Washington University. As the girls approached their teens, there was a good-natured quarreling among them as to who was the best-looking. I would say to each one, "You're pretty in two ways: You're pretty ugly, and you're pretty apt to stay that way." Of course, I was wrong. They all grew up to be stunning beauties.

Annie showed leadership when she was just five-years-old. I had developed strep throat and had a gout attack while their mother was in the hospital for her annual baby delivery. I could hardly walk. Annie took over—cooking, bathing Johnny, Beth, and Pattie, and cleaning. She was too young to drive, otherwise I'm sure she would have done the shopping.

Rita had a refined sense of humor. One morning when she was fifteen, she threw some clothes in an empty guitar case and headed for the highway in four-degrees-above-zero weather. She told the nice elderly couple who picked her up that she had to hitchhike to her guitar lessons because her parents would not drive her there. When we finally located her in Florida, we informed her that we were about to get the FBI on her case. She caught the first plane back and, as she kissed me at the airport, she said in the most carefree manner, "Dad, I want a car for my sixteenth birthday."

The identical twins, Beth (older by two minutes) and Pat, have always been a psychological study. Pat was the tearful one. If you said, "Boo," her tears flowed like the Potomac River. Beth was the tough one. You could sprinkle broken glass in her crib and she wouldn't blink. You don't speak to Beth, you are interviewed by her.

One day in high school, Chris (not pictured) decided to replace the regular cheerleaders at a basketball game. At halftime, he regaled the crowd with his famous Skelly dance. He was asked to leave high school, which was all right with him. Now he dances his way through a successful life.

Johnny has many social graces, and like his siblings, he can carry on a great conversation and play tennis at the same time. As a tennis instructor, he guides his students with the quiet strength he has shown me.

The identical twins, Beth (older by two minutes) and Pat, have always been a psychological study. Pat was the tearful one. If you said, "Boo," her tears flowed like the Potomac River. Beth was the tough one. You could sprinkle broken glass in her crib and she wouldn't blink.

One day in high school, Chris decided to replace the regular cheerleaders at a basketball game. At halftime, he regaled the crowd with his famous Skelly dance. He was asked to leave high school, which was all right with him.

Johnny also has many social graces, for he kissed the Blarney Stone way back when.

Although Lucy and I have been divorced for 25 years, we have managed to keep the children close to each other and to us. And that's even more true after the tragic, sudden death of our youngest son, Lou, six years ago. He was the poet and, all agree, the nicest of us all, the one with the soft smile, a wicked tennis serve, and a gentle soul.

One of the children—probably Pattie, the family poet laureate in residence—handed me the following poem some time ago:

"When passing the doorways of life people ask:

Where are you from?

I tell them

From parents who care.

I've been given life,

and set free.

Thank you, Mom and Dad,

For always loving me."

AMY THARP *Daughter /* | **ROBERT THARP** *Father / Business Owner*

Bookseller | **STACIE** *Daughter*

"We Have Come Full Circle"

When I was growing up, time was often measured by my father's business trips. He frequently traveled, but we stayed in close contact through letters and phone calls. He has always been a truly devoted dad, so the distance never prevented us from sharing a close relationship. Stacie and I always waited eagerly for his return, and he came home with fantastic stories. He took trips everywhere, but his ventures to London held my attention the most. I was fascinated that my father went to such a faraway place. He never tired of answering our questions, and we never tired of asking them.

As we got older, my father traveled less: Stacie and I were the ones coming and going, heading off to college, and taking trips with our friends. It was during my senior year that I realized our lives had come full circle. I spent the fall semester in London and experienced the city of my father's stories. The week before I left England I went to Mayfair, a part of the city he loves. I walked around Grosvenor Square, past the American embassy, and into the Britannia, his favorite hotel. I marveled at the realization that my father had stayed there two decades before. At that moment in the Hotel Britannia, he was right there with me.

As Stacie and I continue to come and go, the stories are now ours to tell. Mom and Dad never tire of hearing them. Time together is not as frequent, but we cherish it all the more. My father is still enthusiastically supportive of our lives. He hates to see us go, but he understands that now is the time for us to explore and make memories of our own. It must be so hard for parents to watch their children grow up and develop lives away from home. I cherish the relationship that my father and I share because it developed from mutual effort, support, and love. As we watched Dad take his trips, we never felt distant from him. We worked hard to stay close, and that is still true today.

DOUG ENGLISH *Father /*

Former NFL All-Pro

RACHEL *Daughter*

BLAKE *Son*

Tuesday the 25th was one of those beautiful springlike days in a Texas February. Claire and I were on our way to the hospital for a scheduled cesarean section to deliver our much-anticipated baby daughter. Of course we were excited, but in the midst of the excitement and anticipation were those nagging I-must-have-been-a-bachelor-too-long thoughts—selfish thoughts. "Say good-bye to spontaneity. No more nights out without arranging for a baby-sitter. Will this little girl turn out to be what I want her to be? I guess my fashionable suburban home will soon look like a toy factory exploded inside it."

After an hour or so of the usual much-too-private-to-have-been-talking-about-that-nonchalantly medical preparations, Claire's doctor presented us with our screaming, gooey, bloody, beautiful daughter. My life changed in an instant. "Who wants to be spontaneous? Arranging for baby-sitters will not be a problem, but why would we want to be separated from the child for even an instant? This beautiful life I now cradle in my suddenly awkward hands possesses the spark to be anything she chooses. Would toy boxes and Disney posters in every room be too much?" She was and forevermore will be the most beautiful thing I have ever seen.

Three years later, God gave us our son. Now I know what Jesus meant when he chose the first two words of his Lord's Prayer: "Our Father." There is a recess in the depths of a father's love that a son can understand only when he has a son. For every sweet, syrupy, tender emotion nurtured in my soul by my daughter arose matching feelings of pride, responsibility, and legacy galvanized by my son.

Five years have come and gone and those emotions, that instant conversion I experienced in the delivery room, have not waned. As I sit in my toy-strewn house, I admit I can now look intently at my daughter for more than five seconds without getting misty eyed. There are even days when I am not completely sure that my son will be Academic All-American, All-Pro, United Way spokesman, become a doctor and find a cure for cancer—but not many.

DAVE THOMAS *Father /*

Founder of Wendy's International, Inc.

LORI *Daughter*

WENDY *Daughter*

KEN *Son*

MOLLY *Daughter*

PAM *Daughter*

"We Weathered the Storm"

My family means everything to me. I can't say that enough. My wife, Lorraine, and I were blessed with five wonderful, talented, and terrific children: Pam, Ken, Molly, Wendy, and Lori. While we all have individual personalities and strong opinions that often differ, we know we are a family when push comes to shove.

Just about every family I know has to deal with an illness from time to time. Thankfully, most are minor but a major illness can really challenge a family. Isn't it a shame that it takes dark days to bring us together? My family joined forces the first time we faced a serious illness—my serious illness. Unfortunately, I was unconscious for much of the time, so I missed out on seeing all the Thomases pull together.

In June 1990, I got really sick. Colds and flu never really bothered me during my life, but this time I was feeling really bad. Constant nausea. Vomiting. The whole thing came on so suddenly, while I was traveling on company business. I was supposed to make a public appearance at a Wendy's charity event, but I couldn't muster enough energy to leave the hotel room.

I flew home and talked to my doctor. I was admitted right away to Ohio State University Hospital. Then things began to snowball. I was alone: Lorraine was traveling in Italy with Pam, Lori, and my daughter-in-law, Kathy. Ken and I were going through a rough stretch and weren't really talking. Molly was in a remote little town in northern Michigan.

When Wendy heard I was in the hospital, she flew straight to Columbus. I told her not to come, that I could manage on my own. Luckily, she didn't listen to me. The doctors wanted to operate and needed authorization. I told Wendy that Lorraine, Pam, Lori, and Kathy should stay in Florence, but again she wouldn't listen to me. She said the family had to be together. I can still remember her pacing the floor with a cellular phone in her hand trying to "Buona sera!" her way through the Italian switchboards to get in touch with Lorraine. Wendy managed to reach Lorraine and Molly, who flew home immediately, and she also talked with Kenny, who headed down to the hospital.

While this was going on, Wendy was the organizer. She and her husband, Paul, were expecting their first child, and she was eight months pregnant. But she took charge: She reassured me that everything was going to be okay and that it was just a question of having the right mental attitude. Still, I was scared to death—scared about what the doctors were going to find. They decided to operate that evening.

Wendy and Molly were there when they started to put me under. Ken arrived just as they wheeled me down to the operating room. I grabbed his hand and said, "Glad you're here, my boy." It was then that the doctors told my family that they couldn't rule out cancer as a cause of my nausea and vomiting.

The operation took nearly four hours. They removed a benign tumor between my large intestine and my liver, and, thank God, I haven't had a problem since.

I learned some lessons from the whole experience. Wendy was right to bring the family together. The family was right to come together and share in making big decisions (it made us stronger and helped heal a few people-to-people wounds).

That close encounter at OSU Hospital was the first major medical scare we had. But it wasn't the only one.

In December 1996, I suffered a heart attack in the middle of the night. Thank God I wasn't alone. Lorraine and Lori were at home with me, and they did all the right things. They called 911; the ambulance arrived within minutes and whisked me off to the hospital. The doctors decided I needed to have bypass surgery, but we had to wait a few days until my body could better handle it. Again, my family came together. For five days we waited side by side. I drew comfort from them, and I know they drew strength and comfort from each other.

The surgery went well, and I'm feeling better than ever. And my family weathered another storm, coming out of it stronger and closer than ever.

That's what family means: You can have disagreements, but when you need a shoulder to lean on, you're always there for each other. Past hurts and disappointments are forgiven, and the love that brings you together gets stronger and stronger.

People say that I had a pretty rough start in life. They might be right. I was adopted as a baby, and my adoptive mother died when I was five. My adoptive father moved from city to city looking for work, and he remarried a few times. I never felt like I was really part of a family. I didn't feel like I really belonged.

When I married Lorraine, I wanted my children to have the stability and love of family that I didn't have. To her credit, Lorraine did most of the child-rearing while I worked and built a business. Many times she was both mother and father. That our five children turned out to be successful, caring adults with families of their own is a tribute to her.

In the early 1990s, I decided to do what I could to help others who didn't have a family of their own. We created the Dave Thomas Foundation for Adoption, which is dedicated to educating prospective parents about adoption and helping waiting children find homes. Lorraine and I are also very active in the Children's Home Society of Florida. This outstanding group helps children who are neglected or abused get the treatment they need and find permanent homes if needed.

When I look back over my life, I am proud of what I've accomplished. But what stands out most for me is family—my own special family, and those I help create through the adoption process. That's my greatest accomplishment.

"A Gift From the Universe"

My son's name, Gautama, literally means "the enlightened one." It was given to the ancient prince who attained enlightenment ages ago as the Buddha. I believe my son is one of the leaders in the coming generation.

My wife and I told Gautama at an early age that although we had begotten him, he does not belong to us. He was a gift from the universe, and we have been his caretakers for the time being. It has been our privilege and honor to have that role.

I believe we are all here for a purpose and each of us has a unique gift to give to others. In accordance with this principle, Gautama was never told that he needed to get good grades in school or go to the best colleges. He was only told that he must find out what his unique talents are and put them to the service of humanity. Today, Gautama is a student at Columbia University with a passion for religious studies and literature.

When Gautama was just six, we spoke about how we come alone into this world and leave it alone, but in between we meet as travelers for a few precious moments. My son put it this way: "We came here on different trains, and we have encountered each other at the train station. Before we embark on separate trains again, on separate journeys, let's have fun!"

Gautama told me, "We have met before, a long time ago, on a bridge near a mountain in Tibet, and we were in the habit of switching roles." We are all ancient souls, and indeed it is our destiny to play an infinity of roles. But we are not the roles we play. The alert witnessing of these roles is the first step on our journey of awakening.

I am beginning to recognize that our children are our greatest teachers. It has been said that the child is father of the man. I am convinced that this, indeed, is true.

SHIRLEY "LITTLE DOVE" CUSTALOW-McGOWAN

Daughter / Mother

CHIEF WEBSTER "LITTLE EAGLE" CUSTALOW *Grandfather*

SAMUEL "RUNNING DEER" *Son*

TRACEY ELIZABETH "GENTLE SPIRIT" *Daughter*

RACHEL "TALKING MOON" *Daughter*

"The Great Spirit's Love"

My grandfather, the late Chief George Forest Custalow, gave me my mission in life when I was five-years-old. This mission was to travel around in all directions as the four winds blow with the history of our people. I must look and see non-Indian people through the eyes of the Great Spirit and share our heritage with the Great Spirit's love.

I did not understand this mission at such a young, tender age, but I remembered every word. I remember even today, Grandfather's face, his voice, and the touch of his hand as he held my hand in his. He is ever with me.

After Grandfather went to be with the Great Spirit, I would ask my father, Chief Webster "Little Eagle" Custalow, so many questions about my mission in life. My father, being a man of great wisdom, would say, "Be still, my child, and wait. The Great Spirit will reveal all you need to know in his timing." I learned great patience as a child. I was taught the history of my people of the Powhatan Nation on the Mattaponi Indian Reservation by my father. I had so many questions as I grew older still and learned my heritage and the skills of my people, such as how I would know when to start my mission, how I would know where to travel, how I would be able to see non-Indian people through God's eyes, and share my heritage with God's love.

My father and mother always reminded me, that as I traveled this beautiful land that God created, to always stand with dignity, respect, and honor for our people and to treat all people, their heritage, and their property with the same respect with which we would want them to treat our people.

Thank you, Dad and Mom, for teaching me the importance of prayer at a young age and for teaching me to love and be proud of my heritage. I love you.

"I Taught Him to Work"

"**I**f he doesn't learn how to work, and he steals, it wouldn't be on my part because I have taught him to work."

These are the words I distinctly remember my father saying to the workers on his job when he had me out learning to cut wood on my summer breaks. I was a young boy, and the workers were afraid that I was going to get hurt out there, working with the men.

My father thought it was important that I learn responsibility. I have passed my father's legacy on to my children.

My oldest son, Anthony Bernard Luck, has always been very inquisitive and eager to learn. As a father, I was more than willing to teach him. When Anthony was about five years old, I took him to work with me. He'd sit right there beside me in the truck as I delivered lumber. By instilling the values of hard work and responsibility in him, I set the example and enabled him to provide the same security for his own children.

My middle child, Eric Clinton Brounson, has always loved horses. Once when we were at the fair, he spotted the horses on the merry-go-round and took off running. After searching the fairground for 15 to 20 minutes, I finally gave up and just stood there. It was unbearable to think that I would have to go home, look into my wife's eyes, and tell her that our child was lost. I would have felt like a failure as a father. But when I turned around, there was Eric, looking up at me.

Crystal Latasha Brounson was and always will be my baby girl. She has always looked on things I considered small and unimportant as being special because they showed fatherly love to her. When I shaved, she had to shave also, so I allowed her to with a bladeless razor. And at night, I put her water in the freezer to crystallize. She looked upon that as a special treat for her.

My youngest is now 18, and if I had to do it all over again, I wouldn't hesitate. When I look at my children, I thank God for giving me strength and guidance in raising them, just as He gave my father.

SPIKE OWEN *Father /*
Former Major League Baseball Player

JACOB *Son*
HANNAH *Daughter*
TRENT *Son*
PRESTON *Son*

"You Can't Fake It"

My dad was always there, and he wanted to be there. His kids were his life, and he took on the responsibility of being a good father. Being with us wasn't a chore; it was what he really enjoyed doing.

Like my dad, I put my family first. I think a lot of what's wrong in the world today is a result of parents not showing their children how to make their way through life. Children need to learn responsibility at an early age. They need to know that there are no handouts and that if there's something you want, you have to work for it. You may not get quite the thing you were working for, but in the long run, if you work hard, you're going to be rewarded for it.

Respect, honesty, sacrifice, hard work, and love are the qualities I learned from my dad. He taught me that in baseball and in life, the one thing you can always do is hustle and give it your best. It's a lesson that I've tried to instill in my own kids. As long as you're trying your best, nobody can ask for more—but you can't fake it.

I always knew I could go to my dad with any problem. If I messed up, I knew that the best thing for me to do was get in touch with him and let him know before he found out through the grapevine. That's the way I hope my kids will be as well. As bad as something may seem at the time, the quicker I know about it and can help, the better it's going to be.

My dad earned the respect of the people around him by the way he lived his life. That's a big word with me—respect—because it's a sign of who you are and what your life stands for. Even though he's gone now, my dad will influence generations to come in our family. Every day, I try to pass on to my children what he taught me.

CHRISTOPHER REEVE *Father / Director* | **ALEXANDRA** *Daughter*

WILL *Son*

MATTHEW *Son*

"We Can Do More Than We Think We Can"

I have been to the edge and back since I nearly died twice in 1995. And the fact is, everything I do with my family, every place we go and everything we see, we share in a new light. That is our triumph. We are happier now than before the accident. I value the present, the here and now.

My five-year-old son, Will, has memories of things we did before: sailing, throwing rocks in the water down by the dock, roughhousing in bed, hiking out in the woods. Now I can't hug him. I can't throw him a ball. I can't help him ride his bike. But I've learned something. It is not about the doing with a child—it is about the being.

A lot of parents say, "Well, I took them skiing, I taught them to play tennis, I did this and that," but they might not have been connecting. They might have been doing the activity, but they're not really in the groove. What I've found is that being with your children is what really counts, connecting with their heart. A lot of times we'll just hang out. Will hangs on my arm, we talk, and he can tell from the look in my eyes how much I love him. That's what really matters.

After the accident, Will got braver. He became fearless. It was as though he had looked his worst fear in the face—that I wouldn't make it—and before, he had nothing else to worry about. Now he uses me as a jungle gym. He climbs on me all the time—when he wakes up from his nap, he'll come right in and jump on me. I'm so pleased. As a father, it would have been distressing if he had been afraid of me because I'm in a wheelchair. I want all my children to continue to count on me. I will always be there for them to lean on.

I've realized that an accident like mine can happen to any of us at any time. I'm glad it happened to me at age 43, and not 22 or 15. That is what really breaks my heart—when I see kids who are struggling with this. I've had wonderful opportunities. I've got a lot of good mileage behind me, and I've got a lot of good mileage ahead of me, too. This is not a road I would have picked, but a lot of times things get picked for you. Either I give in or I say, all right, let's make the best of this.

What I think is a true test of a human being is what you do after something catastrophic happens, whether it's a flood, famine, or disaster in your family. It's what you do after the event. It's what you do with it. I have faith in the best possibilities of human beings—that we can do more than we think we can, that love really conquers every possible problem. Love has been the strongest force in my life—with my wife, Dana, with my children.

The main lesson in life for us to learn is that we're really connected. We're part of a six-billion-member family. We have to really see people. We have to be there for each other. We have to lean on each other. That's how we're all going to make it.

BOBBY NICHOLS *Father /*
Senior PGA Tour Professional

LESLIE *Daughter*

RICK *Son*

CRAIG *Son*

Leslie

There is not a single day that goes by that I don't thank God for blessing me with such a wonderful father. When I was a child, he was away from home a lot, trying to make a better life for our family. But he was always there when I needed him.

I'll never forget the time I had car trouble at the University of Florida. Even though he had a busy schedule, my father drove four hours to Gainesville just to fix my car. At one point, he had car parts spread out all over the parking lot of my apartment complex. I remember my roommates asking me, "Is that your dad out there underneath the hood of your car?" Even today, he takes time out to change my oil or give my car a tune-up.

My father and I have always had a great relationship. He has never been one to pass judgment on the decisions I have made in life, but he has always been there to offer advice and guidance when I needed it most. I know I'll never be able to repay him for all of the gifts he has given to me. I can only hope that he knows how much I love him—and how proud I am to call him 'Dad.'

Rick

Dad is my best friend, my idol. He taught us to respect others as well as ourselves and appreciate what we had. We learned not to ask God for anything but to thank Him for everything. I remember when Dad bought me my first car (a '79 Z28 Camaro!). He said, "Son, you better take care of this, 'cause if you wreck it, you may hurt someone, and you won't get another one!" I still own that car today.

Dad has been at the top of his profession, and he's also struggled, but through it all, his attitude and personality have remained constant. He's always treated others as he would like to be treated, and he taught us to do the same.

To sum it all up, my dad is the most unselfish person I know. (Well, maybe it's a tie with my mother!) I'm his biggest fan.

Craig

Dad is the kind of person you can always count on. He has been there for advice, support, and direction, things that as a young man I needed often and still ask of him today. Golf took him away while we were growing up, but ironically it has enabled us to spend time together when he is home. My brother and I have spent countless hours on the golf course with him. I guess my love for the game came out of love for the man who taught me how to play.

Dad has filled my life with many proud moments, from winning PGA tour events to stopping and helping a stranded motorist along the highway. He is the kind of man who will give you a smile, handshake, and hello in the same manner in which he greets a former president. I have watched him deal with success, yet remain humble, and fail and be grateful for all his good fortune. He has always been kind, caring, and generous, especially to those less fortunate than himself. He strives to be the best person he can, and that is all he has ever asked of his children.

I have learned so much from my father's example. A better role model, I could not have asked for. A better man, I have yet to meet. His love for my mother and their love for their children are the reasons I consider myself one of the luckiest people in the world.

JIMMY YAMAGUCHI, DDS *Father* | **KRISTI YAMAGUCHI** *Daughter /*

Olympic Ice Skater

Our family does things as a team. It's one of our strengths, and it touches everything we do, whether raising funds for a children's charity, or helping our oldest daughter twirl a baton, or working on my son's jump shot, or backing Kristi's desire to skate.

I've always particularly liked doing sports as a family. Even today, most of the Yamaguchis find a way to golf together. Earlier, of course, I encouraged my children's separate interests. Their mom and I saw a lot of baseball fields and basketball courts in those years. We saw a lot of ice rinks, too.

I always tried to emphasize to our kids that they should love whatever it is they set out to do. "If you love what you're doing, if it's worth doing, do it hard," I'd tell my children. "Put forth your best effort, keep trying, and do not be discouraged. The work comes first," I'd repeat over and over. "The rewards come later."

What I made sure not to tell my children was that they had to win all the time, or be the best every time. I wanted them to enjoy their challenges, to do whatever their talent allowed. Kristi always did this. I can't honestly say I ever had to push Kristi to compete or to excel; she just did it on her own. She's not as naturally talented as some other skaters in competition; she wins with motivation and dedication.

I enjoyed watching my girl take top honors, of course, but it was the times when she didn't come out on top that were most touching to me. When Kristi went to her first competition, for instance, she came in second to last. Took my wife four hours to drive Kristi to that competition. Another four to drive back home. Kristi stumbled in dead-tired, looked at me, and said, "Well, it was fun. But I'm not going to come in last again."

Later, as she was beginning her national career, Kristi entered a competition where she did very well, did well enough, in fact, to win. But the final skater came out onto the ice and did such a fantastic job you just knew the judges were going to have to give her the nod. I felt so much for Kristi, watching her watch that performance. The crowd was on its feet, cheering the other skater. I was halfway across the arena from my daughter, wishing every moment I could fly across the ice to be with her, to console her. Every time Kristi competes I remember that moment.

I love her when she comes in last, and I love her when she comes in first. And all the times in between.

CRAIG ANDERSON *Father /*   KATIE *Daughter*
Executive Producer   LIZA *Daughter*

"Doubly Blessed"

People say that if you have twins, you are blessed. The minute Katie and Liza came into my life not a second has been the same. I never used to have time for anything. I was growing and learning and negotiating through life. I thought all the hard work I did was going to make me happy. And it did, but I just didn't have any time left for the really fun stuff. Now that I have Katie and Liza, I am working just as hard. But I also get to bike, hike, water-ski, fish, and play baseball, basketball, and tennis, as well as play dress-up, paint fingernails, braid hair, and go shopping. Do I miss lying in bed on Sunday mornings and reading the *Times* or having long leisurely dinners with friends? Not really. Because it's true: People who have twins are blessed.

WADE F. HORN, PH.D. *Father /*
President, The National Fatherhood Initiative

CHRISTEN *Daughter*
CAROLINE *Daughter*

"Forever Means Today"

At the moment of my first daughter's birth, I—like many fathers—promised her that I would forever and always be a part of her life and quietly told her all the things she and I would be doing together. Two years later, I made those same promises at the birth of my second daughter.

But like many dads, I got busy—busy with a career and making money, busy with friends and buying stuff. Although my love for my two daughters never wavered, my attention did. "Forever and always" all too frequently came to mean "tomorrow."

Then at age 34, I was diagnosed with cancer.

Up until the moment my doctor said the word "tumor," my life had been on the fast track. Magna cum laude college graduate at 20. Ph.D. at 25. Assistant professor at 26. Associate professor at 31. Presidential appointment to be U.S. Commissioner for Children, Youth, and Families at 34. Television appearances on the *McNeil-Lehrer News Hour* and *the Today Show* while still in my early thirties. Success had come relatively quickly. Suddenly, it looked like death might too. It was time to reassess.

As I lay recuperating from surgery to remove the cancer, I thought a lot about my life—about my successes and failures, my accomplishments and regrets. It was then that my earlier promise of forever and always came back to me. And I realized that if I were to die, what I would miss most was not my career, or my money, or my stuff. No, if I were to die, what I would miss most would be those two little girls who each morning before going to school quietly came into my bedroom to give their sick daddy a kiss.

I vowed that whatever happened with my illness, I would spend whatever time I had left paying better attention to my promise of forever and always.

Of course, my attention still wanders at times. I am not perfect. But "forever and always" no longer means "tomorrow." For my two daughters, "forever and always" means "today."

"Listening to Their Dreams"

Fatherhood is opening my mouth and hearing my old man's voice come out. It's being in a hotel in the middle of nowhere and listening to my kids tell me, from thousands of miles away, "I don't remember what you look like." It's hanging up the phone and thanking God for my wife.

Being a father is spending large lumps of time at home in between recording and touring. It's paintball with my son on Sundays and shopping with my daughter. It's realizing that at twelve she's a delight, but she'd rather be with her buddies.

Listening to my children's dreams. I dream too. My daughter loves animals and wants to be a veterinarian. My son, at ten, is talking about being an architect. Of course, at ten, I was going to go into the Army, be a chef, do all sorts of things. I look forward to seeing where they'll both end up.

Fatherhood is supporting their dreams, the way my parents supported mine. I left home when I was seventeen to play music professionally, and they went into hock to buy me a new guitar and amplifier. I hope I'm always as supportive of my kids, even if I think what they're doing is crazy. That's being a father.

GEORGE UCHIYAMA *Father /* | **LINDA** *Daughter*

ELAINE *Daughter*

ROBERT *Son*

"Raising Good Citizens"

Ever since I can remember, I have leaned on the shoulders of both my parents. My father came to America when he was eighteen to seek a new life and fortune. He learned English and went to work, and after six years he had saved enough money to bring a wife from Japan. He exemplified to me that if there is a will, there is a way to overcome life's obstacles.

Because of language and cultural differences, my father seemed to isolate our family from the mainstream of society. We lived where there was no rural electrification and thus no running water, no indoor plumbing, no automatic furnace to heat our house. After school, all of us hurried home to work until dark on the farm, then ate supper only to settle in for the night to study by kerosene lamps.

My parents were poor, but they were very proud people and lived a godly life. My father told us, "America is a great country, and the opportunities here are limitless. Don't be a dirt farmer like me. Go to college and get your education." He taught me that we should set our sights high in everything we do.

They sent all seven of us children to colleges and universities where many degrees and honors were awarded, but neither one of my parents attended a single commencement exercise. All four sons became physicians or dentists, and two of my sisters became nurses. My oldest sister finished business college but unselfishly elected to stay home and help on the farm.

My parents were kind, loving, unselfish, and unassuming individuals whose main aim in life was to raise good citizens, men and women who are self-reliant and have strong family values. My wife, Betty, and I have worked to raise our children with the same values.

Robert

My father struggled through so much to succeed. He was raised on a truck farm in rural Oregon by his father and mother, who were both emigrants from Japan. His father was quite remarkable. He had several years of a high school education in the United States and knew enough English to manage in this new country. He built his own house and delivered all seven of his children. The family survived the Depression by working from dawn to dusk. The children studied by candlelight or by the fire. They slept at night with a rock warmed in the fireplace to keep warm.

Dad was able to go to college at age nineteen after selling a bumper crop of onion seed. Then came World War II. The family was ordered to a relocation camp. They left when they agreed to work as migrant farmers. But still Dad, his brothers, and his sisters persevered in pursuing their education.

I was taught sacrifice and struggle. Dad was loving, gracious, and gentlemanly, but his admonitions were clear: hard work, duty, honesty, and strength of character were what mattered. His expectations were high. With no poverty, Depression, or world war, I should not fail.

Only in America can an immigrant family succeed with nothing but hope for a better life. Dad's father taught him hard work, sacrifice, and the need for education and community service. Dad taught me to trust and have faith in God as well. Thanks, Dad—you are the very best.

Elaine

We always felt loved and supported by our dad, no matter how big or small the task. When my parents took me to Duke my freshman year, my roommate and I wanted to paint our room yellow. Dad helped, not even bothering to change his suit—much to my mother's chagrin. He goes beyond what is asked of him as a matter of course.

Dad taught me the beauty of humility. He is a leader in his profession—he has lectured and taught in Australia, Japan, and Taiwan—but you never hear him brag of his success. Even now, at age seventy-four, they won't let him retire from teaching.

I am forever thankful for the spiritual legacy he has given me. He has been a strong, faithful Christian for as long as I can remember, and God has blessed our family. I am proud of my father and all of his accomplishments and am grateful to him for helping me to become who I am today.

Linda

We are proud to be the second- and third-generation Japanese Americans who wear our heritage on our faces and carry it in our hearts. Hard work, respect for others, education, responsibility, honor for self: These are the values that came from our heritage, our home, our father.

One might ask what "honor" for self means. It is a self-respect that is not proud and a knowledge that when you give, you get. My father, through his actions and through the home he made for us, has taught us these traits.

Our father's background of poverty did not prevent him from rising above it and getting a good education. He became a community leader, a church elder, and an orthodontist who opened a free dental clinic in the inner city.

He showed us that education brings opportunities, and opportunities bring responsibility. We were taught to honor our parents because of the life and love they gave us, our elders for the experience they have to share, teachers like my father because they open the door to the future.

AMY GRANT *Daughter /*

Singer / Songwriter

DR. BURTON GRANT *Father /*

Radiologist Oncologist

"We'll Learn How to Play the Next Hand"

My father is a quiet man. Well, maybe quiet isn't the right word. He doesn't waste a lot of words. He chokes up easily when expressing his gratitude for the good things in this life: his children, his grandchildren, my mom.

When my dad gets tickled about something, he laughs on and on just like a kid. He likes his Mexican food burning hot. He never looks over your shoulder during a conversation to see who else walked into the party.

I remember well from childhood days the smell of his car, the feel of his armchair, the look of his wingtips on a Sunday morning. I remember the feel of my hand wrapped around one of his fingers as we walked.

There was a stretch in my life when the wheels fell off quietly ... privately. The phone call home was difficult for me. I expressed a fear that I would somehow, some way, hurt and embarrass my family because of my own pain.

In the face of all of my confusion, my father said, "Amy, you could never do anything to bring shame on me or your family. Life is hard. If the whole deck of cards that we hold flies into the air and falls to the ground, I'll be there to help you pick them all up, and we'll just learn how to play the next hand."

I love you, too, Daddy.

LARRY STONE, M.D. *Father /*

The President of The American Academy of

Child and Adolescent Psychiatry

MARLA *Daughter*

PAUL *Son*

DAVID *Son*

MARILYN *Daughter*

"Togetherness"

My life as a son of two wonderful parents gave me the motivation to live every moment possible with my children. Since my father's whole world had been as a physician in a rural community, serving all who needed his care, and my mother was totally involved in spreading culture and education to all needy children, I actually spent very little time with either parent. That was not all bad. I felt their protection and their love, and I was active and involved myself. There was always, however, the feeling that I had missed a bit of interpersonal closeness, a one-on-one, or just a parent-and-child togetherness.

I responded to that by doing everything possible with my own children as soon as they were old enough: camp out, hike, swim, mountain climb, fish, hunt, dance, sing, read, ride horses, ski, play baseball, tennis, golf, basketball, football, hockey, volleyball, enjoy animals (dogs, cats, porcupines, monkeys, skunks, coons, javelinas), play board games, river raft, travel, and more. Everything that we could do together, we did.

My son Larry Junior, died at the age of ten after he was hit by a car. That void cannot be filled, but I am grateful for the time I spent with him and glad that I have so many memories of his life to cherish. And the feelings of closeness I share with my other children can and do go on.

Just as I have been a very different parent than my father or mother, so each of my children has been very different than I was as a child. I have loved every minute of being together with each of them. The experiences, the challenges, the sharing, the growing, the loving have made my life complete.

"A Gentle Moment"

Ben...

...The two of us need look no more... My father is more than a wonderful man. He's a really cool woman. I have known my dad most of my life and what is most memorable about this quirky guy is his ability to make strangers feel totally at ease.

We were on an elevator once in a hospital visiting my dad's uncle Bill, who at the time was very sick. Just my father and me, and this lady we didn't know, standing in the elevator at Cedars Sinai Hospital. The woman was crying—evidently going through the loss of a loved one. Ben looked at this grieving woman, made eye contact, and asked, "Has anyone told you how beautiful you look today?" She looked at him as if some strange angelic maitre d' had dropped in just to ease her pain for a few seconds. Her eyes widened appreciatively. "No." A beat. "Thank you."

All three of us got teary. It wasn't like he'd hit on her or anything—my dad saves his intense sexual passion for my mom. It was merely a gentle moment of human kindness.

That's the gift my father has given me. And it's probably the reason I spend so much time in elevators. Besides my love of Muzak.

CHRIS EVERT *Daughter /*
Tennis Champion

JIMMY EVERT *Father*
JEANNE *Daughter*
JOHN *Son*
DREW *Son*
CLARE *Daughter*

"You've Got to Play Every Day"

My dad was very old-fashioned in his beliefs, but he was very modern in his view of his role in the family. He wasn't going to let my mom have the kids all day while he went to work and then see us for only two hours at night. The reason he got us to play tennis was that he wanted us all to be together.

When Mom went with me to Europe, Dad stayed home and just slid into the role of Mr. Mom. He'd cook for four kids, take them to school in the morning, go to work, pick them up, take them to the tennis courts, give them their baths, and put them to bed. He did everything, and he had no problem with that.

My dad is still working to this day. He never quit his job, even though I earned a lot of money. I have seen other situations in which the whole family goes on tour, and the kid supports the family. My father always worked, and he always supported our family.

He was very strict when we were growing up, but very loving. We had a little fear of him, but we also obeyed him. I listen a lot more to my kids. My parents were so busy with five children, trying to work and raise us with no help, that they felt they had to establish order and control. We weren't running around like wild Indians like a lot of kids nowadays—like my kids are nowadays!

There's also more humor in my house. When we were growing up, our home was very serious. As a consequence, all the kids in our family are hilarious now. Even my dad's more relaxed now. He cracks up all the time.

My dad was my incentive for tennis, and he was my hero growing up. I never had a poster of anybody on my wall. My dad was my inspiration.

"Every Memory Is Keener"

"**W**ho wants to go to the diner?" Daddy yells from our parents' bedroom. I can hear his loud footsteps as he walks excitedly toward my bedroom door. As it is a Saturday morning just before ten, I am, of course, still deep under the covers.

"T, come to the diner with me," Daddy says from the foot of my bed. I grumble something about getting in the shower.

"Mick, are you up?" he asks while walking through my bathroom into Michael's adjoining room.

Michael and I are both home for the weekend from our respective law schools. While getting up this early on a Saturday is not the norm for us, the prospect of a delicious breakfast at our favorite diner on Connecticut Avenue is enough to make us crawl out of bed with some vigor.

Within twenty minutes Michael, Daddy, and I are standing on our front porch breathing in the cold, crisp air on that sunny winter morning. We have a brief discussion (argument) about who is going to drive, but within ten minutes Michael is parking his car in front of the diner, and we hop out.

As we walk into the crowded diner, the aroma of bacon, coffee, and pancakes floats through the air. All of the tables are taken, so Daddy sits between Michael and me at the counter. We give cursory glances to the menu, but we each know what we want.

"My beautiful daughter will have corned beef hash with eggs over easy, and I'll have the same," Dad tells the waiter behind the counter. "My knucklehead son will have pancakes, bacon, and scrambled eggs. And we need three OJs."

Dad turns to Michael and in the sweetest voice he can muster, he says, "Sonny, are you gonna hook me up with some of your 'cakes?" When Michael refuses, Dad orders a side of pancakes for himself.

As the waiter brings us our three glasses of orange juice, Dad reaches over Michael to grab the newspaper sitting on the counter. He gives each of us a section. We read and comment on the stories until our breakfast is served. Then all conversation ceases. It's time to grub.

Life will never be the same,

But in one way it will be better:

Every memory is keener.

The feeling of holding his hand

The advice in times of indecision

His sloppy kisses

The never-ending support

The warmth of his hugs

His belief that we are the most beautiful and brilliant children

The pride in his eyes

When this photo was taken, seven-week-old David was still a week from his scheduled appointment to breathe the Earth's atmosphere. He wasn't supposed to be here just yet. That he came to us eight weeks prematurely, contributing less than three-and-a-half pounds to the planetary mass, has altered the gravity of his mother's and my life in ways we could scarcely imagine. I guess he figured he had the tools already, had gotten what he needed from the womb, might as well go outside and stretch the lungs. For reasons yet unknown, he is in a hurry to get on with his life.

As with all premature infants, or "preemies," his birth at 32 weeks' gestation dissolved any notions we may have had about the idyllic full-term pregnancy: the dramatic build-up to labor and delivery, followed by a storybook return to the nest. For five weeks, our "nest" was a neonatal intensive care unit, which was long on technology but short on the comforts of home. No big Plexiglas window for the family to crowd around to ogle the new addition, no magical trip home, scared and excited, the day after his arrival. But if we have been robbed of some essential aspect of early parenthood, one reward has more than compensated: bonus time with our boy. For David it has been bonus time with the world, a sneak preview of coming attractions. He has no qualms about taking on the world at a young age. As parents, we're preemies too. And we don't have any qualms either.

In spite of his size, David is not as fragile as you might think. His physical strength seems out of all proportion to his stature, and his feistiness and willpower—evident in all manner of purposeful *grrs*, coos, and wrinkled foreheads—hint at untold ambitions already taking shape. A ravenous appetite is an indicator of the six-foot-plus Bavarian and Scottish genes on both sides of his family. (Only 62 inches and two and a half hundred pounds to grow before he catches Dad!) His inquisitive nature shows itself in tiny black eyes that scan the room like miniature video cameras, pausing momentarily to consider lights, sounds, faces. There are early signs of a reasonable and agreeable nature, though it's conceded that his mother has not yet had an opportunity to insist he finish his broccoli.

David will in time become a Boston Red Sox fan, an affliction that has plagued three generations of Hornfischer men before him. He will be taught to play chess as well as baseball, just in case his efforts to hit a curveball prove to be as fruitless as his father's (a slow-pitched softball is another story). David will spend plenty of time outdoors discovering new and exciting ways to wear holes in the knees of his jeans. He will be encouraged to develop his father's bloodlust for reading. If the video generation has become alienated from ink on paper, who is to say what the virtual reality generation will think of that arcane pastime? All the more reason to cultivate it.

David will pursue his own dreams as well. As we have recently found, they can take surprising and wondrous twists. But if he is in a hurry to start chasing his dreams, evidenced by his early arrival, all his parents want to do now is slow down and savor these special extra moments, this bonus time with our remarkable three-and-a-half-pound little man.

"I Always Knew He'd Come"

When I think of my dad, I'm three-years-old again, waiting anxiously at the kitchen door for him to come home from work. He used to leave in the morning before I woke up, so the end of the day was our time together. I'd get so excited when he came in, carrying his black tin lunch pail shaped like a half moon. He was strong and gentle and warm, and he'd hug me, and we'd all sit down to supper, eating homegrown vegetables from our garden and talking about our day.

It's funny: When my mom wanted to adopt me, my dad wasn't too keen on the idea. He was happy with the two little boys they had, and he didn't think they needed another mouth to feed. But when he held me, that changed. We've been inseparable ever since. Even today, I can't wait to talk to him on the phone. I love being around him. I can't wait to see him.

All my life I've never had to wonder if my dad was going to be around or not. He's always been there for all of his kids. He gets so excited about anything that happens to us, and he's there to help us, whether we're moving or building something or whatever we're doing. I don't know what I'd do without him.

He still surprises me, too. Two Christmases ago, he wanted so much to give all of his children something real special that he came up with himself, but he didn't feel there was anything he could buy that I couldn't afford to buy for myself. So he gave me a paper bag. On the outside of the bag, he wrote, "There's a real big hug inside this bag for you. Anytime you need one, reach in and get it." Never-ending hugs: That's my dad.

As I'm about to give birth to my first child, I'm grateful to my parents for showing me what family means. Being a family is more than just having a daddy or a mommy or getting together on holidays. It's being there. They've always been there when we were bad. They've always been there when we were good. They've always loved us, with unconditional love.

I guess the reason the memory of waiting for my dad to come home from work is so special is that I always knew he'd come. He never let me down. I waited every day for him to come home, and he always came home. I've always had the comfort of having a dad who was there for me and still is—every step of the way.

TEXAS STATE SENATOR	STEVE *Son*
ROYCE WEST *Father*	TARA *Daughter*
	ROYCE JUNIOR *Son*
	REMARCUS *Son*
	ROLANDO *Son*
	RODDRICK *Son*
	BRANDON *Son*

"Wisdom Is the Principal Thing"

Steve, Tara, Royce, Remarcus, Rolando, Roddrick, and Brandon are the light of my life. I have held each of them in my arms, protecting and nurturing them. Each has provided me with memorable moments: Steve's recognition and acceptance of God as his personal savior; Tara, my one and only daughter, in her odyssey to discover her true talents; Royce obtaining his Eagle Scout rank; Remarcus' graduation from high school; Rolando hitting a 216-foot home run; Roddrick standing before an audience at school reciting his lines; and Brandon, the leading scorer on his soccer team and one of the best readers in his class.

My experiment with the old institution of parenthood has led me to instill the following ideals in my children:

1) The Book of Proverbs, Chapter 4, Verses 5, 6, and 7 states:

"Get wisdom, get understanding; forget it not; neither decline from the words of my mouth. Forsake her not (wisdom), and she shall preserve thee; love her, and she shall keep thee. Wisdom is the principal thing; therefore get wisdom, and with all thy getting get understanding."

2) Fatherly advice for those children who have become adults, at least in their minds:

"I will always love and support you with all of my resources, as long as I have input in your decision-making process. I am not asking you to do everything I tell you, but I do ask you to listen. If after my input you decide to go in another direction, I will still love you, but don't expect me to support your decision with my resources."

3) Some lines from a poem, the title of which I can't remember:

"Excuses are moments of nothing, they build bridges to nowhere, those that use these tools are masters of nothing."

Although each of my children is at a different stage of life, I hope and pray that I have equipped them with the necessary value system to traverse the twists, turns, peaks, and valleys they're sure to encounter.

RICHARD LINKLATER *Father / Director* | **LORELEI** *Daughter*

"Improvise and Learn from Each Other"

I wasn't really prepared for fatherhood. Being the youngest in my family, I hadn't been around children and just didn't have much of a feeling for them. It was all so alien to me that I sort of felt sorry for parents on some level—I also thought it was corny when proud parents huddled and went on about their children, showing pictures and all that.

Any insecurities I might have had, combined with my obvious emotional gaps, started disappearing incrementally once my daughter Lorelei was on the way. I'll never forget the flood of emotions when first hearing her heartbeat and later seeing her in the ultrasound. But life had not prepared me for her arrival—easily the most intense, profound moment of my life. Being there when she entered the world, struggling for her first breath, eyes open, determined, took me to a level I never knew existed. Only thirty-seconds-old, my deepest primordial instincts kicked in and I knew we were bonded for life. From this same place I have continually experienced my deepest joys and emotions—all brought on by a smile or expression from her.

I've spent my entire adult life obsessing on movies and can't help but find parallels between being a parent and making films. Despite all rational and meticulous plans, eventually you're operating on pure instinct, making moment-to-moment decisions that are hopefully inspired but could be screwing things up permanently. Ultimately, if you've been true to yourself, you accept it as the best you can do at the time under the given circumstances and make your peace. Eventually you come to feel you were just a medium for the bringing forth of something that had a preordained destiny all along and will have a life very independent of you, whether you like it or not.

Lorelei has a spirit and destiny that are far beyond me. The greatest gift I've had is to experience the world through a new perspective in relation to her. But I'm especially glad that in the continuum of our lives, we have no scheduled completion date, and that we can improvise and learn from each other for life.

KRIS DAVIS-JONES *Daughter /* | **DANIEL JONES** *Father /*

Television Journalist | *Businessman*

"Earning the Title"

January 20, 1987, is the day I adopted my dad. I was a sophomore in college. Kris Davis became Kris Davis-Jones. Most people believe I'm a modern woman tacking on her married name. My name is an everyday tribute to a man who wasn't there when I was born or even when I was conceived. Unlike most fathers, Dan Jones did years of work before he earned the title.

My dad's three other daughters carry his DNA, but I inherited his independence, work ethic, stubbornness, and dislike of all things sticky. He and my mother were married when I was ten, but it was my adolescence that bonded us. During the craziness of my teenage years, I leaned on my dad and sought comfort in his calm voice. I didn't always like what he said, but he taught me that the crisis of the moment was never as huge as it seemed.

Mom was definitely the caretaker. Dad still can't find the kitchen or the laundry room, but he's great in a crisis. Of course, I've given him plenty of practice. I broke my ankle four times and wrecked cars just as often. He's also got that defining dad quality—the ability to figure out why my checkbook won't balance in exchange for Hershey's Kisses. Somehow I think he'd do it even without the chocolate.

We are what society calls a "step" family, or the more politically correct "blended" family. Those terms are strange to me. Many people who've known me for years never realize we don't share blood. I've never felt less his daughter because I wasn't born to him. In fact, the opposite is true. Every day for years, he's chosen to care for me, and every day I write my name, I honor him for it.

We are father and daughter, not by blood, but by choice.

ABE BROWN III *Son /*

Actor / Producer / Reporter

ABE BROWN JR. *Father /*

College Track Coach

"You Have Passed It On to Me"

How does he do it? That is a question I have asked myself about my dad all my life. He may not know this, but he is batting a perfect .1000 when it comes to giving advice and being there for me in times of need. How is he always right? Is it possible that he has secretly been reading a book titled *Mystify Your Children With Perfect Advice for the Rest of Their Lives*—or is it God-given wisdom? I don't know! Sometimes I compare the mystery of my dad always being right to the UFO phenomenon. There has to be a logical explanation, but what is it?

My dad is a successful college track coach, but he still made sure, no matter what the situation, that he was always there for me to lean on. I remember a time when my world became unstable. I went off to college, felt very much alone, and at the same time, my parents were moving away from the house where I grew up. It was hard for me to experience my parents' moving—children are the ones who usually leave, not parents. My dad told me two things. One, I could always come home; and two, everything would be just fine. He was right—again.

I realize how fortunate I am to have a dad who cares, who takes the time to be there, and who loves me unconditionally. Dad, Coach Brown, I think I know your secret—in fact, I think you have passed it on to me. And for that, I say thank you.

KIX BROOKS *Father /*   **ERIC** *Son*

Singer / Songwriter   **MOLLY** *Daughter*

"A Heart That Trusts and Believes"

Riding the tour bus home, I find myself lost in the anticipation of seeing my children again. Once you have kids, it's hard to remember what made your life important before they came along. My wife, Barbara, and I had a ball when it was just the two of us, but somehow my long-ago ambitions seem selfish, my accomplishments shallow, in comparison to the way I view things now.

Molly and Eric are two very different personalities—she is very analytical in her approach to life, and he pretty much shoots from the hip—but God has blessed them each with a warm and caring heart. A heart that trusts and believes can amplify disappointments in life, but emotions should not be dull. I have a strong feeling they both are destined to contribute something very special to this world. They certainly have contributed a lot to mine.

As a parent, I believe the best I can do is set a good example. Someone once said, "If you screw up raising your kids, nothing else really matters." Truer words were never spoken.

BETH MARIE HALVORSEN *Daughter /* | **ROBERT HALLQUIST** *Father*

Lutheran Pastor

When I decided to enter a Lutheran seminary, it was still not common for a woman to consider being a pastor. But while others in my family wrestled with my choice, it was my father who spoke simple words of encouragement to me. Throughout my life, I have talked more with my mother and brothers than with my father, but it is his quiet words of support and advice that have guided and shaped me the most.

I am proud of my father. He ran our family-owned trucking business in such a way that he had what he called "a clear conscience at bedtime." He remains disciplined in his exercise and diet, respecting the body God gave him. (At 81, he still regularly walks-runs five miles and lifts weights!) I am also proud of my father's outlook on life. I see it in his smile. I hear it as we laugh at his one-liners. I notice it in how he gives people and events a positive slant. And when I disagree with him, I appreciate how he genuinely listens to me, quietly asserts his viewpoint, and simply asks me to respect his decision.

And all the while, I know that he loves me and believes in me.

"The Adventures Never Stop"

True fatherhood in the professional rodeo world takes a tremendous effort on both the father and the child. Being a professional calf roper requires a lot of time away from home with an unbelievable amount of traveling. It also means having to keep my priorities in order. My top priority happens to be my family.

My children enjoy being on the road with me, which gives me a chance to share incredible adventures with them. Whether it's Houston, Cheyenne, Calgary, Reno, Las Vegas, or New York, I get an opportunity to see and do many memorable things with them. The adventures never stop: driving by Custer's last battlefield, stopping to stand on exactly the same spot where the battle was fought, or driving down the coast of California and trying some bodysurfing, or driving through Yellowstone National Park to watch Old Faithful blow, or passing by Mount Rushmore and Clif saying, "Dad, how can I get my face up there?" I am a lucky man to have these special opportunities to see the wonder of God's creations through the eyes of my children.

My children also like to rope, which gives me a chance to teach and practice with them. There is no pressure put on them to rodeo. They are free to choose what they want to do, and they are encouraged to strive for success in whatever they try.

When I'm away from my family, I call as much as possible, at least five times a day. I know the kids' schedules so I can be sure to talk to them every day. I hate being away from my family, and I realize that the time we are together must be quality time. We have mutual respect and admiration for one another, so time together is not taken for granted.

Fatherhood and rodeos can be a tough combination. It takes communication, understanding, and patience.

Winning eight world championships and reaching the pinnacle of my sport were goals set and achieved. But my life would be far from complete without the love and support of my children.